Beyond the
Solar System:
from Red Giants to Black Holes

Steve Parker

First published in Great Britain in 2007
by Wayland, an imprint of Hachette Children's Books

This paperback edition published in 2009
by Wayland, an imprint of Hachette Children's Books

Wayland
338 Euston Road, London NW1 3BH

Editor: Nicola Edwards
Designer: Tim Mayer
Consultant: Ian Grahan

British Library Cataloguing in Publication Data
    Parker, Steve
    Beyond the solar system. - (Earth and space)
    1. Outer space - Juvenile literature
    I. Title
    523.1

ISBN : 9780750249966

Wayland is a division of Hachette Children's Books,
an Hachette UK Company.
www.hachettelivre.co.uk

Cover photograph: Emission nebulae contain many young, hot stars and glow brightly.

Photo credits: Bettmann/Corbis: 5, 34; Natalia Bratslavsky/Shutterstock: 6; Chris Butler/SPL: 21; John Chumack/SPL: 16, 19; Dennis di Cicco/Corbis: 8; ESA: front cover; ESO: 1, 14, 15, 26, 42; ESO/SPL: 10; Mark Garlick/SPL: 23, 24, 36; Victor Habbick Visions/SPL: 35; David A. Hardy/SPL: 12; Herman Heyn/SPL: 20; Hulton Deutsch Collection/Corbis; 37; Jodrell Bank Observatory, University of Manchester: 44; Douglas Kirkland/Corbis: 30; Matthias Kulka/Corbis: 4; Marshall Space Flight Center/NASA: 33; NASA: 9, 11; NOAO/SPL: 17, 25, 28; Max Planck Institut fur Radioastronomie/SPL: 40; Paul Rapson/SPL: 39; Detlev van Ravenswaay/SPL: 27; Roger Ressmeyer/Corbis: 7, 29, 41; Royal Greenwich Observatory/SPL: 45; Royal Observatory Edinburgh/AATB/SPL: 13; John Sandford/SPL: 22; Erich Schrempp/SPL: 31; Courtesy of Ben Simons, University of Sydney Vislab © CSIRO: 43; Eckhard Slawik/SPL: 18; Universal/The Kobal Collection:38; X Ray Astronomy Group, Leicester University/SPL: 32.

Contents

Our Place in Space

Our home planet, Earth, seems huge. But it is very small compared to the biggest planets that orbit, or go around, the Sun, such as Jupiter. And Earth is tiny compared to the Sun itself. Yet even the Sun is just a speck in the true vastness of deep space.

Earth and Sun

Every tiny star in the night sky is a colossal ball of light and heat, and there are untold billions of stars stretching into the depths of space.

Planet Earth is about 12,750 kilometres across. If you could drive around it at motorway speed it would take you almost 15 days and nights non-stop. Our nearest giant object in space is the Sun. It is so enormous that it could hold 1.3 million Earths inside. And it is so far away that if you could drive the same car through space it would take 150 years to reach the Sun.

Our Solar System

The Solar System consists of the Sun, the eight planets that orbit it, the moons of these planets, and many other objects that are affected by the immense pulling force of the Sun's gravity, such as asteroids and comets. To drive in the car to the farthest planet from the Sun, Neptune, would take 4,500 years. Past Neptune there are even more Solar System objects in the region known as the Kuiper Belt, such as the 'dwarf planet' Pluto. To drive there would take over 7,000 years. Such distances may seem huge. But they are truly almost nothing compared to what is outside the Solar System.

Studying space

For thousands of years, people have gazed at the stars and wondered how far away they are, what they are made of, and whether their patterns and movements have any meanings. From the 1600s astronomers have peered upwards through ever more powerful telescopes. And from 1957 we have launched spacecraft that tell us yet more about deep space and the amazing objects and events there. We now know that all the stars we see twinkling in the night sky are far beyond the Solar System.

Galileo was keen to show others his telescope. Here the poet John Milton takes a look.

Space Facts

Telescopes through the ages

● The first person to study the night sky through a telescope was the Italian scientist Galileo Galilei, from 1609.

● Telescopes opened up a previously invisible 'new world' of thousands of stars that are too faint to see with the unaided eye.

● The first telescopes were refractors, using curved pieces of glass called lenses that bent or refracted light rays.

● In about 1668, English scientist Isaac Newton designed a reflector telescope using bowl-like curved mirrors to bounce or reflect light.

● A telescope's size, such as 2.4 metres, usually refers to the main mirror or lens that collects the light.

Patterns in the Stars

In ancient times there were no electric lights for homes, streets and buildings – just flickering candles or fires. Nights seemed much darker and longer, and stars appeared to shine more brightly. People gazed upwards, saw shapes and patterns, and invented tales of gods and monsters who lived and died among the stars.

Stars on the move

From the time of the Sumerians more than 6,000 years ago, astronomers recorded patterns in the stars. They saw how the stars seemed to arc across the night sky, and also how they changed their angle above the horizon with the passing seasons. Now we know that these changes are caused by the Earth spinning around every 24 hours and also travelling on its yearly path, or orbit, around the Sun.

Mayan astronomers studied the movements of stars from the observatory at Chichen Itza.

Charts and calendars

From about 4,000 years ago the Egyptians and Babylonians recorded the positions of stars and used them to predict events such as floods and when to plant crops. In ancient China and India, people took great interest in the stars. Almost 2,000 years ago the Maya people of South America constructed special buildings, which we would now call observatories. They studied the positions of the Sun, Moon and stars, to work out very accurate calendars and plan their events through the year.

How do we know?

Tycho Brahe

Before the telescope, Danish astronomer Tycho Brahe (1546-1601) measured the positions of more than 750 stars with great accuracy. His star catalogue book *Rudolphine Tables* was published 26 years after his death by his former assistant Johannes Kepler, himself a famous astronomer.

Constellations

Many of these ancient people imagined that certain patterns or layouts of stars portrayed spirits, gods, monsters, animals and people. They gave the patterns names and made up stories about them. More than 2,000 years ago, Ancient Greek astronomers identified patterns that we still use today, called constellations.

Mapping the night sky

Most people no longer believe those ancient tales. But constellations are a useful way of mapping the night sky and giving different areas names. For example, Orion the Hunter is roughly above Earth's equator and so it can be seen from most parts of the world. Above the North Pole is Ursa Minor, the Little Bear. Other famous constellations include Pegasus the Winged Horse, Draco the Dragon, and the longest constellation, Hydra the Water Snake.

The four bright stars, upper left, form the Southern Cross constellation, or Crux.

Space fact - or fiction?

Astrology

● Astrology deals with how the Sun, Moon and stars can affect human lives and behaviour. Some people say it can predict the future.

● Astrologers use the names of constellations as 'star signs', such as Pisces, Capricorn and Scorpio.

● Most scientists argue that astrology has no basis in fact.

Our Galaxy: The Milky Way

For hundreds of years, astronomers were puzzled by the faint band of light that arches through the night sky, called the Milky Way. Today we know that stars are clustered into massive groups called galaxies, and that the milky band of light is a 'side view' of inside our own galaxy.

What are galaxies?

Galaxies are vast regions of stars, gas, dust and other space objects grouped together, and surrounded by the immensity of empty space. A single galaxy contains millions of stars, and there are millions of galaxies. Our Solar System is in a galaxy called the Galaxy (with a capital 'G') or the Milky Way Galaxy.

Spiral shape

If you could look at our Galaxy from far outside, you would see a central ball-like bulge surrounded by a flat, thin disc. The disc has several bright curving arms giving a spiral-like shape. Around the main disc is an even larger faint glow or halo.

Space Facts

The spinning spiral

- Our Galaxy is not still. It is spinning around like a giant top.

- This means the Solar System is zooming around the Galaxy's centre at more than 200 kilometres per second.

- The Solar System takes about 225 million years to go around the centre once.

The wispy, faint glow of the Milky Way is the central up-down band in this night sky.

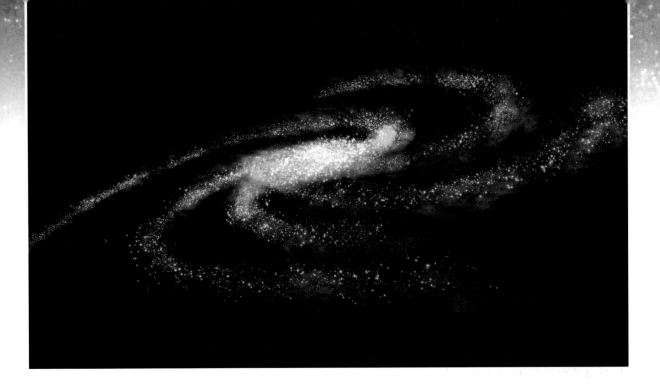

When we gaze at the Milky Way in the night sky, we are looking at billions of stars within the thickness of the disc. If we look to either side we are gazing 'above' and 'below' the main disc, where there are far fewer stars before we can see through to the outside.

One of the most common shapes for galaxies is a spiral galaxy, which spins around in space.

Light-years across

The Galaxy's main disc measures up to 100,000 light-years across. A light-year is a common measure of distance in space. It is the length that a beam of light travels in one year. Nothing travels faster than light, at 300,000 kilometres per second. This means a light-year is about 9.46 million million kilometres. So the Galaxy measures almost one billion billion kilometres across.

Our place in the Galaxy

The Galaxy's four main arms, curving from its centre, are called Perseus, Crux-Scutum, Norma-Cygnus and Carina-Sagittarius. There are also several minor arms branching from the main ones. Our Solar System is in one of these minor arms, the Orion Arm, just over one-half of the way from the Galaxy's centre to its edge.

SPACE DATA

The size of the Galaxy

● The Galaxy's central bulge is around 30,000 light-years across.

● The main disc around the bulge is 1,000 light-years thick.

● The faint halo extending from the main disc is up to 400,000 light-years across.

● The total number of stars in the Galaxy is around 200 billion.

Galaxies Beyond Our Own

Our Galaxy is far from alone. There are thousands of other galaxies which we can see easily with ordinary telescopes – and billions more stretching into the depths of space.

'Blobs' in space

Dotted across the night sky are faint patches, 'blobs' or 'smears' of light known as nebulae (meaning misty or formless). In the 1920s US astronomer Edwin Hubble (1889-1953) used a powerful new telescope to study the Andromeda Nebula. He saw that cloud-like parts of it were actually made of individual stars, and he reasoned that it was a galaxy outside of our own. Hubble went on to study other galaxies and put forward the idea that the Universe is getting bigger.

How do we know?

Hubble's telescope

Edwin Hubble's new telescope, which he began using in 1923, was at Mount Wilson Observatory in California, USA. It had a mirror 254 centimetres across, bigger than any other telescope of its time. This allowed him to see individual stars in what, through smaller telescopes, looked like a vague mist.

Light from the spiral Southern Pinwheel galaxy (M83) takes 15 million years to reach Earth.

Galaxies glow with different shapes and shades of light, depending on how they formed, their distance and the kinds of stars in them.

Types of galaxies

Hubble devised a system for grouping galaxies according to their shapes.

- Elliptical galaxies vary from almost spherical (ball-shaped), to egg-shaped, to long and slim.

- Spiral galaxies have a bulging centre with curving arms spreading outwards.

- Barred spiral galaxies resemble spiral galaxies, but the arms have a straighter section where they join to the central bulge. Straight sections of arms on opposite sides of the bulge form a 'bar' across the galaxy. Our own Galaxy is a barred spiral.

- A galaxy which is just a bulge with no arms is known as lenticular (lens-shaped).

- Galaxies with no clear shape are known as irregular.

Within a galaxy, the stars are held relatively near to each other by their huge pulling forces of gravity. The different shapes of galaxies are probably due to the way they formed billions of years ago.

Space Facts

Radio galaxies

- Most galaxies give out several kinds of energy, such as light rays and radio waves. Radio galaxies produce much more radio energy than normal galaxies. Some give out no light, as far as we can detect.

- The huge radio galaxy Centaurus A (NGC 5128) is quite close to our own Galaxy. It's 'only' 15 million light-years away.

- Seyfert galaxies have faint spiral arms around a very small, bright central region or nucleus. The nucleus sends out many kinds of energy, including light, radio waves and even X-rays. These galaxies are named after US astronomer Carl Seyfert (1911-1960), who discovered them in 1943.

Clusters of Galaxies

Stars are clustered into vast groups called galaxies, with millions or billions of stars in each galaxy. In a similar way, galaxies are not spread out evenly through space. They are also clumped together, forming groups of galaxies called clusters. And the clusters are in groups too, known as superclusters.

Nearby galaxies

The nearest large galaxy to our own is the Andromeda Spiral, code-numbered M31. 'M' stands for Messier, after French astronomer Charles Messier (1730-1817) who compiled an early list of about 100 nebulae and other space objects. M31 is the 31st object in Messier's original list. It is sited in the constellation, or pattern of stars, called Andromeda. At 200,000 light-years across, it is about twice as large as our own Galaxy. The Andromeda Spiral is some 2.5 million light-years away from us, and it is the most distant object visible to the unaided eye.

This faraway view of the Local Group shows our own Galaxy (lower right) and the Andromeda Galaxy (top left).

Space Facts

The Local Group and beyond

● The cluster of galaxies nearest to our own Local Group (see page 13) is the Sculptor Group. This is about 6-14 million light-years away. Its main galaxy is NGC 253, a large spiral galaxy. There are also many fainter spiral galaxies in this cluster.

● The Large and Small Magellanic Clouds are about 160,000 and 200,000 light-years away. They are named in honour of the Portuguese sailor Ferdinand Magellan. He described them in 1519, as he used the stars to navigate while attempting his round-the-world voyage.

Galaxy clouds

Two nearer but smaller galaxies are known as the Large and Small Magellanic Clouds (see page 12). They are classed by astronomers as dwarf irregulars, being quite small and randomly shaped. The Magellanic Clouds are actually 'companions' of our Galaxy. They move around or orbit our Galaxy, in the way that planets orbit the Sun. In 2003 a galaxy was discovered even closer. This is the Canis Major Dwarf, 25,000 light-years away from Earth.

The Local Group

Our Galaxy (the Milky Way Galaxy), the Magellanic Clouds, the Andromeda Spiral, and another large galaxy known as the Triangulum Spiral (M33), are all members of a small galaxy cluster called the Local Group. This is because it is in our 'local' region of space. The Local Group contains about 20 galaxies, although most of these are dwarf ellipticals, or dwarf irregulars like the Magellanic Clouds.

The Virgo Cluster shines brightly in the middle of the Local Supercluster of galaxy groups.

Clusters and superclusters

Clusters of galaxies are gathered into even larger groups known as superclusters. The Local Group cluster is near the edge of an incredibly vast supercluster known as (predictably) the Local Supercluster. This is more than 100 million light-years across. At its centre is the gigantic Virgo Cluster, or Virgo-Coma Cluster. The galaxies within this cluster are spread through the star constellations of Virgo and Coma Berenices. The Virgo Cluster is about 50-60 million light-years away, and contains up to 2,000 observed galaxies.

Birthplace of the Stars

Stars do not carry on for ever – they have 'lives'. They are born, they grow older, they change size, they become brighter or dimmer, and eventually they die. Their lives are very long, lasting millions or billions of years.

Star lives

The Horsehead Nebula shows up as a dark, light-absorbing cloud against the brighter star background.

All across the Universe, stars are continually forming, growing, shining, and then exploding or collapsing and fading away. Using telescopes, from Earth we can see stars in different stages of their lives, and so work out their typical life cycles.

In the beginning

Most stars form from vast, thin, wispy clouds of dust and gas in space, called nebulae. Occasionally something disturbs a nebula, such as shockwaves from an exploding star nearby. Slowly the dust and gas in the nebula begin to clump together. Each tiny part is attracted to the others by its own pulling force of gravity. Smaller clumps merge into bigger ones by this process of gravitational collapse.

As the collapse continues, regions of the nebula become denser, with more matter or substance in an increasingly small place. The main matter is the tiniest particles, or atoms, of the gas hydrogen. This is the lightest and most common substance in the Universe. The denser regions of the nebula get hotter as the matter becomes more squeezed and compacted. These hot, dense regions are known as protostars.

Herbig-Haro 34 (HH-34) is a complicated mass of whirling gas jets and streaks that are gradually forming into stars, in the Orion Nebula.

Switched on

What happens next depends on the mass, or amount of matter, in the protostar. In many cases it clumps together so densely that hydrogen atoms start to merge or fuse together. Four of them fuse to form one atom of a slightly heavier gas, helium. As this happens huge amounts of energy are given off, mainly as heat and light.

Fusion happens when the centre of the protostar reaches a temperature of about 15 million °C (degrees Celsius). Then billions of four-hydrogens-to-one-helium reactions begin every second. At this stage the protostar becomes a true star – that is, a space object that converts matter to energy and gives this out in forms such as light and heat.

Space Facts

Types of nebulae

● Emission nebulae contain many young, hot stars and glow brightly. An example is the beautiful, shimmering Orion Nebula (M42), visible with the unaided eye below the 'belt' in the constellation of Orion.

● Dark nebulae have few or no stars and show up as dull shapes against the brighter background of other stars and nebulae. An example is the striking Horsehead Nebula, at the eastern end of Orion's 'belt'.

● Planetary nebulae are formed from individual stars.

What Starlight Tells Us

The light from a star looks like a white pinpoint. But scientists use various machines and methods to study starlight in great detail. This reveals how hot the star is, what it is made of, how it was born, and how it will die.

A rainbow of colours

The light from our nearest star, the Sun, looks bright and white. But if it shines through certain objects, it is split up into a whole range of colours, known as the spectrum of sunlight. We see this spectrum naturally when sunlight is split by millions of raindrops. We call it a rainbow and we describe its colours as red, orange, yellow, green, blue, indigo and violet.

Stars in the constellation Cepheus shine with different colours when seen through a powerful telescope.

Any type of light can be split by passing it through a triangular block of clear glass or plastic, called a prism. A prism-based device called a spectroscope can be attached to a telescope, to split and analyze the light from an individual star (see panel).

How do we know?

The spectroscope

In astronomy, a spectroscope is used to split light from the object being viewed, into its many colours or spectrum. In a typical spectroscope, light from the telescope eyepiece shines through a narrow slit, then through a lens which makes its rays parallel. A prism splits it into colours, then a second prism enlarges a small part of the spectrum under study. Another lens focuses the coloured rays onto a screen.

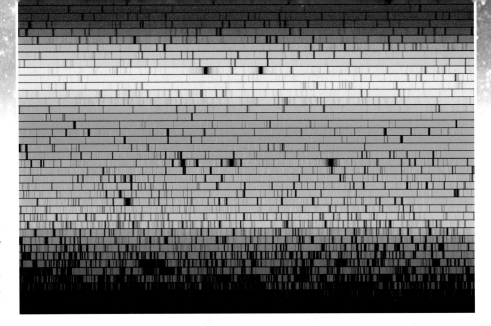

The spectrum of the star Arcturus (type K) has hundreds of absorption lines, indicating tiny amounts of different chemical substances.

Space Facts

Star types

- The main code letters for star types are O, B, A, F, G, K and M. The types are ordered by temperature, from the highest to the lowest.

- Hottest are type O 'blue stars', with a surface temperature up to 60,000 °C.

- In the middle are type F 'white stars' with a surface temperature of about 7,000 °C.

- Coolest are M-type 'red stars', with surface temperatures as low as 2,000 °C.

- Numbers 1-9 are added to the letters to break these broad categories into smaller groups. So A0 are the hottest stars in group A, and A9 are the coolest. Sirius the 'Dog Star' is A1. The Sun, with a surface temperature of about 6,000 °C, is classed as a G2 yellow dwarf star (see page 22).

Different colours

Astronomers have studied the spectra of thousands of stars, and found that they are not all the same. They vary in the brightness and the proportions of the colours making up the spectrum. Cooler stars make more red light, while very hot ones emit more blue light. Stars can be grouped according to the type of spectrum they produce. The type of spectrum is, in turn, linked to the surface temperature of the star. A code letter and number show the type and temperature (see panel).

Colours and lines

A star's spectrum often has dark lines on the continuous background colours. These are known as absorption or von Fraunhofer lines, after German scientist Joseph von Fraunhofer, who noticed them around 1812-14. The lines are caused by the presence of tiny amounts of certain chemical substances in the star, such as oxygen, silicon, iron and titanium. So a star's spectrum shows not only its temperature but also its chemical make-up.

Bright or Dim?

Which star is the brightest? That depends – on whether we mean the brightest star when seen from Earth, or the star which gives out the most light. In turn, this depends both on measuring how far away a star is, and on measuring how bright it is – which astronomers call magnitude.

Apparent magnitude

There are several types of magnitude, and they apply not only to stars but to other space objects like planets and moons. Apparent magnitude is how bright a star appears when seen from Earth. It does not take into account the distance of the star from Earth. So a very bright star far from Earth may look dimmer than a much duller but nearer star.

Using apparent magnitude, the brightest star in the night sky is Sirius A, the Dog Star. It is about 8.6 light-years away in the constellation of Canis Major, the 'Great Dog'. Next comes Canopus in the constellation Carina. But Canopus is about 313 light-years away, which is more than 35 times farther than Sirius A.

The brightest star (after the Sun) seen from Earth, Sirius A, shines brightly at the upper right, in the Canis Major constellation.

Absolute magnitude

A truer idea of a star's light output is called absolute magnitude. It is a measure of brightness if the star could be viewed from a standard distance of 32.6 light-years. If Sirius A and Canopus were both moved to this distance from Earth, then Canopus would be dozens of times brighter than Sirius.

A strange scale

The magnitude scales run from negative to positive – that is, the brighter an object, the more negative its magnitude number (see panel on page 18). The Sun is so overwhelmingly brilliant that it has an apparent magnitude of minus 26.7. The full Moon's brightness is minus 12.7, and the planet Venus reaches minus 4.7. Only a few stars are magnitude minus 1. The scale then runs past zero to plus numbers. As these increase, the stars appear dimmer and dimmer.

Arcturus (Alpha Bootis) is the fourth brightest star in the night sky. (Its spectrum is shown on page 17.)

In both the apparent and absolute scales, a star of magnitude 1 is not twice as bright as one of magnitude 2. It is 2.512 times brighter. Likewise a magnitude 3 star is 2.512 times brighter than a magnitude 4 star. This means a star of magnitude 1 is 100 times brighter than one of magnitude 6 (2.512 x 2.512 x 2.512 x 2.512 x 2.512 = 100).

How Far is a Star?

The stars of the Southern Cross look near to each other, but some are much farther away than others.

Stars that look faint from Earth might not be shining dimly. They could be very bright stars, but far away. Also two stars that seem close together might not be close at all. One could be much, much farther from Earth than the other. This is why it is so important to measure distances in space.

From there to here

There are several ways of measuring the distances of stars and other space objects, as seen from Earth or from other places, such as the centre of our Galaxy. Astronomers need to know these stellar distances so that they can work out features such as a star's absolute magnitude, which is how much light it gives out.

Parallax shift

One method of measuring stellar distances is based on parallax. This is when nearer objects appear to cross in front of farther ones as the observer changes position. For example, if you hold up a pencil at arm's length and view it first with one eye, then the other, the pencil seems to shift or jump across the background. This is due to parallax. In a similar way, as the Earth goes around the Sun from one side of its orbit to the other, the nearest stars seem to move across in front of the very far ones.

SPACE DATA

The Earth's nearest stars

Star	Distance in light-years
Proxima Centauri	4.2
Alpha Centauri A, B and C (Rigil Kentaurus)	4.4
Barnard's Star	6.0
Wolf 359	7.8
Lalande 21185	8.3
Sirius A, B	8.6
Luyten 726-8A, 8B	8.7
Ross 154	9.7
Ross 248	10.3

Astronomers draw a triangle from two observation points, on each side of Earth's orbit, out to the star they are looking at. Knowing the angle of the star from each observation point, and how much it moves across the background of other stars, they can calculate the star's distance.

Cluster method

Another method, used for more distant stars, is the moving cluster. This tracks the motion of stars in a cluster over several years. In reality they all move together and stay much the same distance apart. But when seen from Earth, they seem to be coming together or getting farther apart – like a swarm of bees that seems to grow bigger as it approaches. The movement speed of the stars is also determined by red shift (see pages 34-35). These various measurements combine to give each star's distance.

(see pages 34-35)

As a planet orbits, stars seem to shift their positions, as the nearest ones move across the farthest ones. This parallax shift helps to calculate a star's distance.

How do we know?

Bessel's estimate

German astronomer Friedrich Bessel (1784-1846) was first to work out the distance to a star using parallax shift. The star was 61 Cygni, in the constellation of Cygnus, the Swan. Bessel's measurement of 1838 was 10.3 light-years. Modern measurements taken by more accurate devices give 11.4 light-years.

Dwarves and Giants

Once a star forms, its fate depends mainly on how big it is. Small stars tend to change their matter to energy fairly slowly, so they shine dimly but for a long time. Bigger stars use up their matter faster and may grow so huge that they explode.

Sun-type stars

A star with the same mass (amount of matter) as our Sun is a typical smaller or dwarf star – a yellow dwarf. It has a life of about 10 billion years. The Sun itself formed around five billion years ago and is halfway through its existence. Over the next five billion years it will gradually use up its hydrogen 'fuel' and swell to hundreds of times its present size. It may become so huge that its surface reaches Earth – if our planet has not been burned away by then.

Red giants

As they get bigger, the Sun and stars of similar size will also become slightly cooler and redder. The surface temperature will fall to about 3,500 °C compared to the former 6,000 °C. At this stage in its life the star is called a red giant.

In the constellation of Orion, the pinkish-white star at the upper left is Betelgeuse, a red supergiant.

Space Facts

Shedding shell

Inside a red giant, all the hydrogen 'fuel' is eventually changed by fusion into helium. Then this helium becomes the fuel, until it too runs out. Then the star begins to shrink and cool. As it does so it pulsates and sheds or 'puffs off' its outer layers of thin gases. Through a telescope the puffed-off layer of gases looks like a misty disc around the star, and is called a planetary nebula.

Red and brown dwarves

- A space object less than about 1/20th the mass of the Sun is too small for fusion reactions. It may glow but only very dimly, as a brown dwarf, due to gravity collapse (whereby its own gravity, the pulling force of all the matter it is made of, makes it shrink smaller and smaller).

- Stars not quite large enough to be yellow dwarves, like the Sun, are known as red dwarves. They can last up to 100 billion years and are the most common stars in our Galaxy.

Fade and die

Stars like the Sun continue to shrink until they reach a stage where they are small, dimly-glowing white dwarves. Their matter is packed into a ball only a few thousand kilometres across. This is so heavy or dense that a bucket of it would weigh a million times more than a bucket of water. The dimly-glowing dwarves continue to fade away into cold, dark 'dead stars' known as black dwarves.

The Sun, upper right, is tiny compared to a blue supergiant star on the left. The inset shows the Sun compared to its largest planet, Jupiter.

Star Pairs and Groups

Space Fact

Orbital times

How fast do multiple stars orbit around each other?

● One of the fastest binaries is RX J0806.3+1527 in the constellation of Cancer the Crab. Its two white dwarf stars, each the size of Earth and only 80,000 kilometres apart, orbit each other every five minutes.

● At the other extreme, in some binaries the two stars take thousands of years to orbit each other once.

Algol has one cool, orange star and one smaller, brighter, hotter white star.

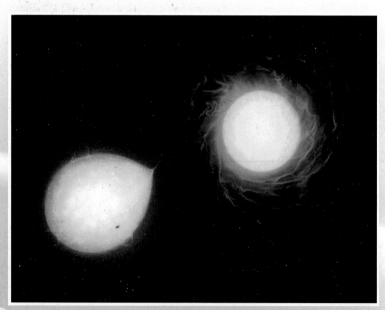

The Sun is a single, lone or solitary star. It has no nearby companion. But most stars are not solitary. They have partners nearby – one, two or sometimes more.

Two stars close together are known as a binary or double star. Three are called a triple star, and so on. The nearest stars to Earth, Alpha Centauri A, B and C, form a triple system. Sometimes there are more than 10 stars all near each other.

Complicated orbits

The movements of these multiple stars can be very complicated. In a binary formation the two stars orbit each other, like two tennis balls joined by a length of string. They revolve around their common centre of gravity – the place where their gravities combine. If the stars have equal mass, this point is midway between them. If one star is much bigger, the common centre of gravity is nearer to it.

Stars that wink

From Earth, we see some binary stars side-on, so that one passes in front of the other, then the far one comes around to the front, and so on. If one star is darker than the other, then as it passes in front of its brighter partner, it eclipses or blocks out the light. So the binary seems to shine bright, then dim. This is called an eclipsing, flashing or 'winking' binary. A famous example is Algol (Beta Persei, see panel page 25).

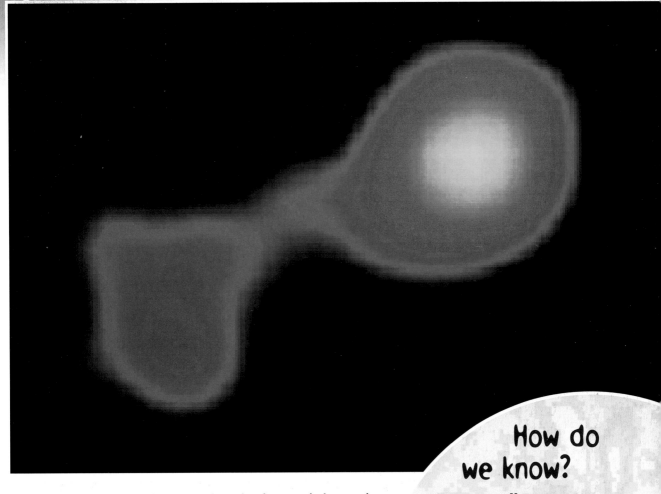

Seen through an X-ray telescope, Mira A is a huge red giant and pulses in brightness. Its partner Mira B is a tiny white dwarf.

Brighter, dimmer

Our Sun shines steadily. But some stars change their brightness, becoming brighter, dimmer and brighter again (for example, because hot glowing gases expand and flow outwards from the star and are then pulled back in by gravity). They are called variable stars. The best-known are the very bright cepheid variables. They are named after Delta Cephei, the first of its kind to be discovered (see panel). Its cycle of bright-dim-bright takes about 5.3 days. Another type of variable star is the long-period variable. One of the best known is Mira (Omicron Ceti), with a brightness cycle of about 330 days. Like most long-period variables it is a red giant.

How do we know?

An extraordinary astronomer

English astronomer John Goodricke (1764-1786) noticed how Algol changed brightness and suggested it was due to one star passing in front of the other. He also studied Delta Cephei, the first-known of the cepheid variable stars. Goodricke was first to establish that some stars became brighter then dimmer in a regular or pulsing way. As a result of a childhood infection Goodricke could not hear or speak properly, and died aged only 21 years.

Stars with Planets

Our local star, the Sun, has eight main planets orbiting around it. Do other stars have planets? For many years, astronomers did not have powerful enough telescopes and equipment to solve this problem. Now we know the answer is 'yes'.

How do we know?

Astronomers have several methods which they use to detect exoplanets

- They observe the tiny wobbling movements of the star as the much weaker gravity of the planet pulls it around very slightly during each orbit.

- They study the star's light by high-resolution spectroscopy (see page 17), to see if the star is moving under the tiny pull of a planet.

- They watch to see if the star dims by a tiny amount as the planet moves across its face with each orbit. This only works if the planet's orbit has a particular alignment when seen from Earth.

- They use direct imaging, which is viewing an exoplanet by telescope, due to the tiny amount of light it reflects from its parent star.

Exoplanets

Planets orbiting stars other than our Sun are known as extrasolar planets or exoplanets. Scientists had long suspected that other stars had planets. This was partly because the Sun is a very 'average' star, so having planets should be 'average' too.

In 1995 astronomers announced that they had detected a planet orbiting the star 51 Pegasi, in the constellation of Pegasus. This star is similar to the Sun in terms of its size and light output. The first planet to be found around a star takes the star's name followed by the letter 'b' (the star itself is assumed to be 'a'). The second has the letter 'c' and so on. So this first exoplanet, which is about half the mass of Jupiter, was named 51 Pegasi b.

The small dot on the right (b) is a planet orbiting the star GQ Lupi (A) in the centre.

Planets of binary stars have two 'suns' in the sky, and perhaps nearby moons and other planets.

More and more

More discoveries followed quickly as equipment and methods improved. In 2003 came confirmation of an exoplanet which had first been suggested in 1998, orbiting Gamma Cephei (Alrai). By 2006 more than 200 extrasolar planets had been discovered. The study of exoplanets has great importance for another great question – is there life elsewhere in the Universe?

Space Facts

Exoplanets

- Most exoplanets discovered so far are at least 10 times bigger than Earth.
- Many are bigger than our Solar System's largest planet, Jupiter.
- Most exoplanets are nearer their stars, compared to Earth's distance from the Sun.

However these features probably reflect the methods used to find exoplanets, which tend to favour big planets near their stars.

The true size range of exoplanets and their orbiting distances may not be known for many years.

27

Super Explosion

Small stars tend to shrink, cool and fade away. Bigger stars are more likely to live fast and die young – perhaps blowing themselves apart in a gigantic space explosion called a supernova.

Neutron stars

If a star starts out much more massive than our Sun – at least ten times and perhaps up to about 25 times the Sun's mass – it has a very different fate. Like smaller stars it will swell to a red giant and then 'puff off' layers of gas as it shrinks. But instead of then fading as a white dwarf, it will continue to shrink under its own inward pull of gravity. The tiny particles that make up its atoms, known as electrons and protons, merge to form closely-packed particles called neutrons. The result is a neutron star. It has the final mass of the dying star concentrated into an incredibly small body perhaps just 10 kilometres across.

The supernova 1987A shows incredible shock waves of energy blasting out into space after the supergiant star exploded.

How do we know?

Signals from aliens?

The first pulsar, or spinning neutron star, was discovered by the Belfast-born astronomer Jocelyn Bell Burnell (1943-) in 1967. She detected a regular 'beep-beep' of radio wave pulses 1.3 seconds apart. Some people hoped that these signals came from aliens and called the discovery LGM (for 'Little Green Men'). The pulsar is now known as CP1919 / PSR1919+21.

Pulsars

Some neutron stars spin around very fast. As they do so they send out beams of radio and other waves. From afar, the star seems to 'flash' on and off with pulses of radio waves, much as a lighthouse's rotating light beam produces regular flashes of light. These rotating neutron stars are known as pulsars (pulsating stars).

Space Facts

Heaviest of all

● In a neutron star, the neutrons (bits of atoms) are packed so closely that a teaspoonful of them weighs about one billion tonnes. If everyone on Earth was compressed as small as the matter of a neutron star, they would easily fit into the teaspoon.

Pulsars are detected by radio telescopes like the Max Planck dish in Germany.

Supergiants

The biggest stars swell through the giant stage into supergiants. These are hundreds of times larger than the Sun. The red supergiant Betelgeuse is the second-brightest star in the constellation Orion, even though it is 430 light-years away. Betelgeuse is more than 600 times wider than the Sun, has about 15 times the Sun's mass, and shines more than 10,000 times brighter.

Supergiants do not last very long, perhaps a few million years. Then they explode, showering countless bits through space as a wispy cloud or nebula. The explosion is known as a supernova. In 1054 Chinese astronomers recorded a bright supernova whose remnants survive today as the Crab Nebula. In 1987 the brightest supernova of modern times appeared in the Large Magellanic Cloud Galaxy. Called SN 1987A, it was the fate of the star known as Sanduleak −69° 202.

Black Holes

How do we know?
Carry on shrinking

German astronomer Karl Schwarzschild (1873-1916) predicted black holes and calculated the size to which a star must shrink, before it becomes one. This size depends on the star's mass and is known as the Schwarzschild radius.

After a supergiant star explodes, it disappears – literally. The star's remaining central region or core shrinks and collapses under its own gravity, smaller and smaller. Finally it disappears from our view – as a black hole.

Shrinking to nothing

After a supergiant star explodes as a supernova, it still has so much matter that its inward force of gravity makes it shrink, and then shrink further and further. Finally so much matter is packed into such a small place that nothing can escape its gravity, not even light rays. So from the outside, the region looks black.

Anything pulled into a black hole seems to disappear into a bottomless pit, hence the term 'black hole'. During the 1970s-80s English scientist Stephen Hawking (1942-) predicted many features of black holes. Since then many possible sites for black holes have been suggested. But because of their very nature, we cannot 'see' them directly.

How to find 'nothing'

One possible way to detect a black hole is to study certain binary or double stars. If one of these 'stars' is in fact a black hole, then the black hole's gravity can pull streams of gas from its partner. As the two partners orbit, the gas streams around to form a swirling spiral known as an accretion disc. Gas moving in this way becomes very hot and sends out large amounts of X-rays. Finding a binary star with these features is a good sign of a black hole.

Stephen Hawking made huge advances in the study of space, especially black holes.

Floating gases near a black hole are pulled in and disappear.

The first object of this type was Cygnus X-1, detected in the 1970s. Dozens more possible black holes have since been identified. Stellar black holes are left when supergiant stars at least 25 times the mass of our Sun explode. Each black hole has a mass several times that of our Sun.

Space Facts

How big is a black hole?

● The place around a black hole where escape becomes impossible, even for light, is known as the event horizon.

● The place within a black hole where matter is compressed is called a singularity.

● Scientists describe a singularity as 'a point of infinitely large mass and infinitely small size'.

● If all the matter in Mount Everest was compressed into a black hole it would be smaller than the centre, or nucleus, of one atom.

The Depths of Space

Peering into the deepest parts of space is like looking back in time. Light takes thousands, even millions of years to reach us. So we see events out there as they happened long, long ago.

Quasars

In the 1950s telescopes detected incredibly powerful sources of energy, mainly radio waves, coming from very deep space. These amazing objects were far too 'energetic' to be ordinary stars. They were named quasars (QUASi-StellAR radio sources). Gradually some were identified by the light they also produced. But they are so far away that they look like faint single stars. More than 100,000 quasars have now been located.

Supermassives

A quasar is probably based around a supermassive black hole, which contains millions to billions times more matter than the Sun. A 'supermassive' could be formed by the collapse of star clusters, or by many smaller black holes merging together. Its force of gravity is so enormous that it pulls in not just nearby stars but whole galaxies. As these fall inwards they form swirling accretion trails of incredibly hot gases. These give off vast amounts of radio waves, light, X-rays and other forms of energy.

Quasar 3C 273, seen here through an X-ray telescope, was the first to be identified (see page 33).

Space Facts

Ultrabright

- The brightest quasar seen from Earth is 3C 273. It is about 2.2 billion light-years away in the star constellation Virgo and can be seen with a small telescope.

- It shines about 2 billion billion times brighter than the Sun.

The elongated pale area in this image is a cloud of cool gas and dust surrounding a supermassive black hole.

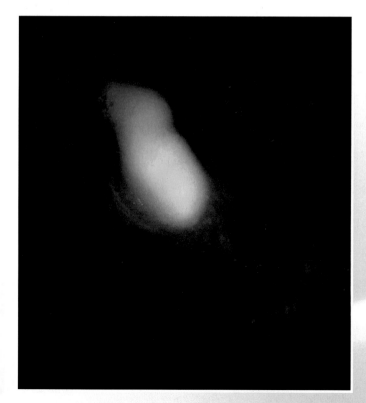

'Eating' galaxies

Most quasars are immense distances from Earth – several billions of light-years away. So we see them as they existed several billion years ago. They 'eat' up to 1,000 stars in just one year, and shine with a brightness hundreds of times greater than our whole Galaxy. They are also moving away from us at amazing speeds, tens of thousands of kilometres every second.

The galactic centre

Many galaxies may have a 'monster in the middle' – a supermassive black hole at their centre. In our own Galaxy (the Milky Way) scientists think this could be the object SgrA*, in the constellation of Sagittarius. It is estimated to contain the mass of more than two million stars like the Sun.

The age of quasars

Why do some galaxies seem to have a supermassive black hole which swallows stars and causes an immense glow, while in other galaxies, like our own, the black hole looks inactive or dormant? Perhaps, for the first few billion years of the Universe, supermassive black holes 'ate' the stars and galaxies around them. Eventually they cleared the local region, ran out of 'food' and became quiet. This is why our own galaxy's supermassive black hole is now mainly dormant. We see the active, shining quasars so far away from us because we see them how they were long ago, when the Universe was young and they were 'hungry'.

The Universe

The Universe (with a capital 'U') can be described simply as everything that exists everywhere – matter, energy, stars, galaxies and everything else, anywhere and everywhere, for all time. Cosmology is the science of the Universe. It deals with events, objects and ideas that many people find totally baffling.

Edwin Hubble is shown looking through the Oschin Schmidt Telescope at Palomar Observatory, California, in 1949.

The expanding Universe

Cosmologists study what the Universe contains, how it works, its past and its fate. One important idea is that the Universe is expanding. This was suggested by US astronomer Edwin Hubble in the 1920s, as he studied galaxies outside our own. Hubble found that the galaxies were moving away from us and away from each other. The farther they are, the faster they move or recede. The main way he detected their motion was using red shift (see page 35).

Space and time

Another important idea in cosmology involves space and time. We are familiar with the normal three dimensions of space – up/down, left/right, near/far. Scientists add a fourth dimension, time, making the 'space-time continuum'. Despite our experience on Earth, where time ticks past steadily, time can actually vary and speed up or slow down.

Worms and spaghetti

These ideas lead to very strange happenings. For example, the faster something travels, the slower time passes. Close to the fastest possible speed in the Universe, the speed of light, time almost stands still.

Also, huge forces of gravity, as found near a black hole, can 'bend' space and time, perhaps into a funnel-like shape. If two funnels join, the result is a space-time tunnel or wormhole. Enter at one end, and you could pop out of the other end in a different place, perhaps far across the Universe – and in a different time too, either past or future. But if you enter the black hole you could be pulled longer and thinner like a piece of string, a process known as 'spaghettification'.

Red shift

When a motorcycle speeds past, its engine note – niiaaaooow – seems to change from higher to lower in pitch. This is known as Doppler shift. It is due to the source of the sound waves, the motorcycle, moving in relation to the listener.

The same effect happens at very high speeds with light waves. If an object moves away from us, its light seems slightly 'lower', which makes it redder than normal. This is known as red shift and is very important in astronomy. The amount of red shift shows how fast the object is receding. An object coming towards us has the opposite effect, called blue shift.

No one knows what a wormhole looks like – but one day a spaceship might enter one.

The Big Bang

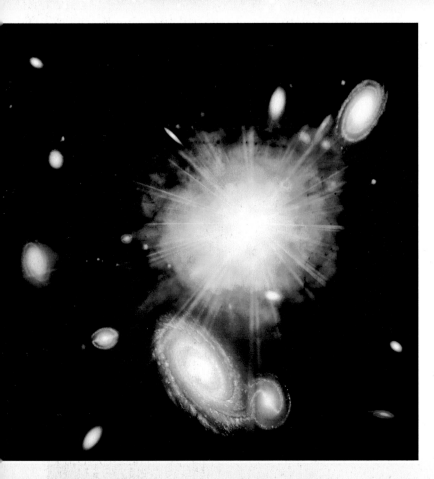

It is possible that everything began with the Big Bang – matter, energy, space and time.

Light takes time to travel through the immense distances of space. So the farthest distance we can see is also the farthest back in time – to the edge of the Universe, and perhaps to its beginning.

Does the Universe have a shape and size? Some cosmologists suggest it is shaped like a ball, disc or doughnut. Perhaps it resembles an immense golfball with many flat faces, like the buildings known as geodesic domes. If the Universe is limited in size, how big is it? Some cosmologists suggest that it is about 40 billion light-years across.

Can the Universe have a size and shape? This implies it has an end or boundary, and so an 'outside'. But if the Universe is defined as everything everywhere, it cannot have an 'outside', since that is simply more of the Universe. Maybe the Universe is simply endless. Or it could have edges yet still be endless, like a videogame where a character goes off one side of the screen and reappears at once on the other side.

The Big Bang

The Big Bang theory suggests the Universe began as an infinitely small, dense point which blew up in an unimaginable event that formed energy and matter. This happened about 13.7 billion years ago, which could be when time itself started. Scientists predicted that the Big Bang would leave 'echoes' or an 'afterglow' of microwaves. The *COBE* (*COsmic microwave Background Explorer*) satellite, launched in 1989, detected these 'echoes'.

Dark forces

Astronomers have shown that the Universe is expanding. Will it slow down and start to shrink again under the relentless force of gravity, to end in a 'Big Crunch'? This idea was popular until the early 2000s. But there isn't enough 'ordinary' matter or energy to explain how stars and galaxies are moving. So scientists suggest 'dark matter' and 'dark energy'. These are named not for their colour, but because no scientific equipment can detect them as yet. They may mean that the Universe grows faster and faster, for ever and ever.

The name 'Big Bang' was suggested as a joke by English astronomer and mathematician Fred Hoyle (1915-2001).

Space Facts

The Big Bang timeline

- Zero – the Universe and time itself come into being.

- Less than one trillion-trillion-trillionths of a second – fundamental forces such as gravity begin as the Universe expands gigantically.

- Less than 1 second – the first atomic particles appear, such as electrons and protons. The Universe has already cooled from 100 billion to 10 billion °C.

- 3 minutes – atomic particles combine into the centres, or nuclei, of atoms.

- Half a million years – whole atoms form and the Universe is mainly a massive cloud of hot gases.

- One billion years – parts of the cloud start to clump together to form early stars and galaxies.

Is Anyone Out There?

Spacecraft have visited all the planets in our Solar System, and some of their moons too, as well as certain comets and asteroids. As far as we know, none of these has any forms of life. Could there be living things beyond the Solar System, in the depths of space?

How do we know?

Project Phoenix

- In Project Phoenix, astronomers around the world monitored radio signals from more than 700 Sun-like stars within 200 light-years of Earth.

- The project used 'spare time' on some of the world's biggest telescopes and ran for 10 years to 2004.

- No signs were found of signals which could come from intelligent life.

Life as we know it

Earth's average temperature means that water is usually liquid, rather than solid ice or a gaseous vapour. Life as we recognize it depends on liquid water. This does not exist, as far as we know, on any other planet, moon or object in the Solar System. Farther away, any kind of star is far too hot for water. So the search for aliens or extra-terrestrial life focuses on planets of other stars – exoplanets. However the small amounts of information we have about exoplanets do not tell us much about the possibility of life there, as yet.

Aliens are popular in stories, television and movies. Some are friendly and cute, like E.T. the Extra-Terrestrial (1982).

People can 'lend' their computer power to SETI, in the quest to find intelligent life in space.

So many stars and planets

Our star, the Sun, is a very average small yellow star. We know it has planets. So the chances are that many similar stars could have planets too. A number of these planets could have Earth-like conditions. On some of these, life may have evolved – perhaps to an advanced stage. There are perhaps 200 billion stars in our Galaxy, and of course there are billions of other galaxies too. With such vast numbers, is there a chance that some planet, somewhere, harbours life?

Making contact

How might intelligent aliens, far more advanced than us, try to make contact? From our scientific knowledge of space, it would probably be by radio or similar waves. Like light, these travel at the fastest speed in the Universe. SETI, the Search for Extra-Terrestrial Intelligence, uses detecting equipment here on Earth to 'listen' for such signals from space. However, distances are vast. Radio waves would take many years to reach us even from the nearest stars, and thousands of years from nearby galaxies – even if they were powerful enough to travel such immense journeys.

How we Observe Beyond the Solar System

No spacecraft have ever visited other stars. The distances are millions of times too far. Seeing into the depths of space demands the world's most advanced telescopes. Yet much of our information comes from telescopes that cannot actually 'see' – that is, they do not detect light.

A spectrum of energy

'Ordinary' telescopes are optical, detecting light rays – like our eyes. But light is just part of a range of rays and waves sent out by stars and other space objects. These forms of energy, made of combined electricity and magnetism, are known as the electromagnetic spectrum. They differ in the length of their waves. Radio waves are longest – a single wave can measure many kilometres. Next shortest are microwaves, then infra-red or heat rays, light rays, ultra-violet rays and X-rays. Shortest are gamma rays, with a billion billion in one millimetre.

Types of telescope

Different kinds of telescopes pick up these types of electromagnetic waves. Some are huge bowl-like dishes. Others look like masts, aerials or antennae with long wires, rows of rods, nets or flat plates. Some of these telescopes are on Earth, perhaps in groups working together, known as arrays. Others are on satellites orbiting Earth. Some are on space probes heading across the Solar System.

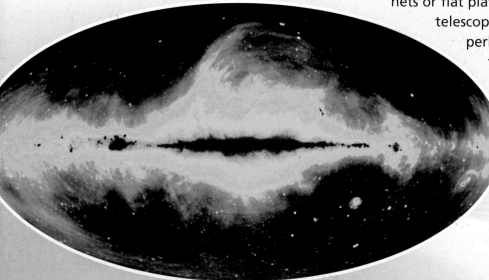

A radio telescope 'sees' the Milky Way as the radio waves it gives off, from blue (weakest) to red (strongest).

Space Facts

Big telescopes

Arecibo The largest single dish radio telescope is a bowl 305 metres across in a natural mountain valley on the island of Puerto Rico.

Keck The biggest optical telescope, with twin curved mirrors 10 metres across, is in Hawaii, USA.

HST The 16-metre-long Hubble Space Telescope orbits Earth 570 kilometres high and has several detectors, including an optical telescope mirror 2.4 metres across.

Parkes This massive 'steerable' radio dish, 64 metres across, is in New South Wales, Australia.

VLA The Very Large Array in New Mexico, USA, consists of 27 separate moveable radio dishes each 25 metres across.

Chandra The Chandra X-ray Observatory satellite orbits up to 133,000 kilometres above the Earth.

VLT The Very Large Telescope at the Paranal Observatory, Chile has four 8.2-metre optical telescopes.

SST The Earth-orbiting Spitzer Space Telescope picks up mainly infra-red rays.

A photograph taken over many minutes shows Australia's Parkes telescope going around.

Incoming information

Each kind of telescope tells us different information. For example, radio telescopes pick up the radio waves of pulsars. Infra-red telescopes sense heat from stars which are too cool to give off much light. X-ray telescopes detect the X-rays coming from the super-hot leftovers of a supernova. Often several telescopes observe the same object and astronomers combine information from them. For example, in 2004 the Hubble Space Telescope and the Keck light telescopes pinpointed a galaxy 13 billion light-years away – towards the observable edge of the Universe.

The Future

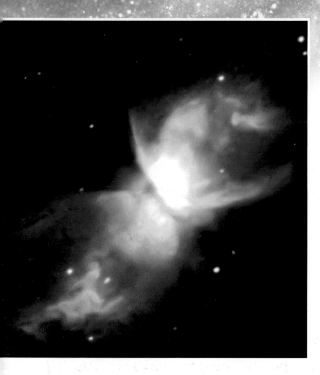

The Butterfly Nebula is one of many space objects that scientists will take years to understand.

We know more than ever about stars, galaxies and other amazing objects beyond the Solar System. But distances in deep space are so gigantic that there is no chance of sending spacecraft there in the foreseeable future. Increasing our knowledge depends on more powerful telescopes, and improved ways of analyzing the information.

After Hubble

The Hubble Space Telescope (HST) orbits far above the clouds and atmosphere which distort our views from Earth's surface. But it was launched some time ago, back in 1990, and its fate is closely linked to the future of the US space shuttle (which maintains and updates the HST). Its planned successor is the Next Generation Space Telescope or James Webb Space Telescope. (James Webb was chief of NASA, the US National Aeronautics and Space Administration, during the 1960s.) With a mirror 6.5 metres across it is scheduled for launch in 2013.

How We Will Know

Projects planned for the medium future include:

- Constellation-X, an array of X-ray telescopes in space.
- The 'black hole hunter' Lisa, the Laser Interferometer Space Antenna.
- The Darwin 'planet-hunting' project of up to eight spacecraft in formation, designed to detect signs of life on rocky Earth-like exoplanets.
- SIM Planet Quest, the Space Interferometry Mission to look for exoplanets.
- SKA, the Square Kilometre Array, plans a spread of radio telescopes dotted about over several hundred square kilometres, with a dense concentration in one smaller area, to give a total detecting surface of one million square metres (one square kilometre).

Alma and Sloan

In 2006 the first radio telescope dish was installed for ALMA, the Atacama Large Millimetre Array. It is on a dry plain high in the Andes Mountains of Chile, where the effects of the Earth's atmosphere are less. Its eventual network of up to 50 dishes is expected to discover a new galaxy every few minutes.

The SKA, Square Kilometre Array, *could have many small radio telescopes in rows.*

The Sloan Digital Sky Survey began in 2000. It uses a 2.5 metre telescope on Mount Apache, New Mexico, USA. Sloan aims to record more than 100 million stars, galaxies, quasars and other space objects in about one-quarter of the sky. It is part of the process of mapping the Universe. In its first five years, phase 1, Sloan detected nearly 200 million celestial objects and measured the spectra of more than 675,000 galaxies, 90,000 quasars, and 185,000 stars.

Times ahead

Each new telescope answers some of our questions, yet uncovers new and exciting mysteries. Will people ever travel into deep space? Light has the fastest known speed. Even so, it takes many years to reach us from nearby stars, and thousands of years from a nearby galaxy. Even our speediest spacecraft travel at only a tiny fraction of light speed. Unless scientists make some incredible breakthrough in time travel, perhaps by harnessing wormholes, then humans are unlikely to leave the Solar System and reach the stars just yet.

Space Facts

Space predictions

● In the 1970s a group of scientists and engineers dreamed up project Daedalus, a massive robot starship as big as an ocean cruise liner, with a fusion power rocket. It could travel at one-seventh the speed of light. But it was only a dream.

● Our nearest stars in the Alpha Centauri system are about 40 million million kilometres away. Using today's rocket and space probe technology, such as ion drive propulsion, a craft would take about 10,000 years to reach them.

● Even at the speed of light, a trip to these 'nearby' stars and back would take up to 10 years.

● But science predicts that a starship approaching the speed of light would become so heavy, there is not enough energy in the Universe to keep it going faster and reach the speed of light.

Timeline of Discovery

13.7 billion years ago The Big Bang, when the Universe and everything we see, know and study – including perhaps time itself – came into being.

About AD 150 At the time of Ancient Rome, Ptolemy compiled a huge book of observations of the Sun, Moon, planets and stars, called the *Almagest*, which dominated European astronomy for 1,000 years.

1054 Chinese astronomers recorded the supernova whose remnants now form the Crab Nebula.

1609 Galileo Galilei was the first scientist to study the night sky with the newly invented telescope, observing many stars as well as the Moon and planets.

1627 The huge star catalogue *Rudolphine Tables* was published, compiled by Tycho Brahe and completed by Jonannes Kepler.

1774 Charles Messier published his first list of star clusters and nebulae, and his 'M numbers' for these objects still used today.

Grote Reber (1911-2002) was first to build a radio telescope dish, in 1938. Later he built larger versions.

1838 Friedrich Bessel was first to calculate with reasonable accuracy the distance to a star, 61 Cygni.

1864 John Herschel produced the first GC, General Catalogue, of star clusters and nebulae.

1888 Johan Dreyer published the first version of the NGC, New General Catalogue, of star clusters and nebulae; it is still being expanded.

1929 Edwin Hubble announced the results of his study of the Andromeda Nebula, showing it was extragalactic (outside our own Galaxy).

1938 The first telescope dish was built by Grote Reber.

1943 Carl Seyfert described the types of galaxies named after him.

1959 Guiseppi Cocconi and Philip Morrison described how civilizations might communicate across space using radio waves, starting the idea of SETI, Search for Extra-Terretrial Intelligence.

1963 The first quasar, 3C 273, was discovered.

1963 The world's largest telescope, the Arecibo radio dish, was completed in Puerto Rico.

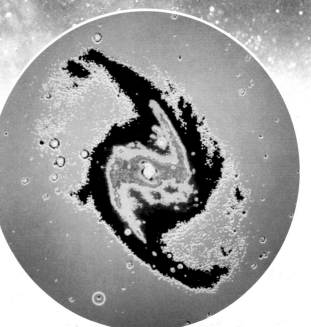

Information from X-ray telescopes is fed into computers to make pictures of stars and galaxies, like the barred spiral galaxy NGC 1365.

1967 Jocelyn Bell (now Bell Burnell) was first to detect a pulsar, or fast-spinning neuron star.

1971 Tom Bolton identified object Cygnus X-1 as probably a black hole.

1987 The brightest supernova of recent times was seen in the Large Magellanic Cloud.

1992 Information from the COBE satellite showed microwave radiation throughout the Universe as the 'echo' or 'afterglow' of the Big Bang.

1993 The Hubble Space Telescope was successfully repaired, extending its working life by many years.

1995 The first exoplanet – one orbiting a star other than our Sun – was discovered, going around star 51 Pegasi.

1998 The term 'dark energy' was coined.

2004 The Chandra X-ray Observatory satellite gathered new evidence for dark energy by confirming that the Universe's expansion is getting faster.

2006 Hubble, Chandra and the National Radio Astronomical Observatory combined to show a galaxy cluster whose central supermassive black hole has a mass of one billion Suns.

Glossary

absolute magnitude The brightness of a star when seen from a standard distance of 32.6 light-years.

apparent magnitude The brightness of a star when seen from Earth, which depends partly on the distance of the star from Earth.

binary star Two stars very close together, usually both orbiting each other.

black dwarf The final phase for many smaller stars, when they become very small, cold, dark and 'dead'.

black hole A place in space where matter is squeezed so tight and small that it has incredible density and gravity, and not even light rays can escape.

constellations Groups of stars that form patterns in the night sky.

dwarf star A smallish star, or a star which is in the smallish phase of its life.

exoplanet (extrasolar planet) A planet which orbits a star other than our Sun.

Fraunhofer lines Dark lines in the continuous band of rainbow-like colours made by splitting a star's light into its spectrum.

galaxy A massive group or clump of stars with empty space around them. Our own galaxy is known as the Galaxy (with a capital 'G') or the Milky Way Galaxy.

gravity A pulling or attracting force possessed by all objects, mass and matter.

Kuiper Belt A ring-like area of the Solar System beyond the planet Neptune.

light-year A measure of distance, being how far light travels in one year, which is 9.46 million million kilometres.

mass Matter or substance, in terms of the numbers and types of atoms or other tiny particles.

moon An object that orbits around a planet, but that is not part of a planet's rings.

nebula A huge wispy, flimsy 'cloud' of dust, gases and other tiny particles floating in space.

neutron star An unimaginably dense, heavy space object made of the particles called neutrons, formed after a big star shrinks enormously due to its own gravity.

orbit The path of one object going around another, such as a planet around the Sun.

planetary nebula Shell-like 'puffs' of gas thrown out by a giant star as it shrinks towards the end of its life.

probe A spacecraft launched into space to send back information about objects.

pulsar A type of star called a neutron star that spins around very fast, emitting beams and waves of energy such as radio waves.

quasar (quasi-stellar radio source) A region where a huge black hole is sucking in whole galaxies, which send out incredible amounts of radio waves, light, X-rays and other energy.

red dwarf The smallest and most numerous type of star, which is smaller than our Sun, and relatively cool.

red giant A large star, much bigger than our Sun, which glows with red light signifying it is not that hot.

red shift When a star or similar object appears redder than it really is, because it is moving away from the observer.

star A space object that changes matter to energy and gives this off as light, heat and other kinds of waves and rays.

supergiant The largest type of star, hundreds of times bigger than our Sun.

supernova An exploding star that blasts itself to pieces.

white dwarf The last light-emitting phase of life for many stars, when they become smaller and cooler.

Further Information

Books

Astronomy: Discoveries, Solar System, Stars, Universe
Carole Stott
Kingfisher, 2003

The Big Bang (Great Ideas of Science)
Paul Fleisher
Twenty-First Century Books, 2005

National Geographic Encyclopedia of Space
Linda K. Glover
National Geographic Society, 2005

The Solar System and Beyond (Fundamental Physics)
Gerard Cheshire
National Geographic Society, 2007

Websites

imagine.gsfc.nasa.gov/docs/science/know_l1/active_galaxies.html
Part of NASA's Imagine the Universe series of web sites and pages.

heasarc.gsfc.nasa.gov/docs/binary.html
Animation and explanation of a binary X-ray star, with links to similar items on black holes and supernovae.

www.kidsastronomy.com/
A large site with plenty of fun information on many topics including deep space, galaxies, quasars and black holes.

www.schoolscience.co.uk/flash/bang.htm
Interactive timeline of the Big Bang and what followed.

Organizations

National Aeronautics & Space Administration (NASA)
Organization that runs the US space program.
www.nasa.gov

SETI Institute
The Institute's mission is to explore, understand and explain the origin, nature and prevalence of life in the Universe.
www.seti.org

Jet Propulsion Laboratory (JPL)
Centre responsible for NASA's robot space probes.
www.jpl.nasa.gov

European Space Agency (ESA)
Organization responsible for space flight and exploration by European countries.
www.esa.int

Hubble Space Telescope
The Earth-orbiting telescope has its own web site about its many amazing discoveries and the breathtaking pictures it has taken.
hubblesite.org/

The Official String Theory Website
Explains string theory and its involvement in cosmology, black holes, fundamental particles, mathematics and much more besides, with basic and advanced descriptions.
www.superstringtheory.com/

Index

Numbers in **bold** indicate pictures.